Praise for *Escape velocity*

"Deborah Sosin's cleverly conceived *Escape Velocity* is a potent mix of intimacy, wit, and mounting angst over the inevitability of aging, offered in crisp, seventy-word capsules of remarkable honesty. Sosin portrays a fascinating, surprising life, ending on a perfect note of hope and resilience."

—**Dinty W. Moore**, author of *Between Panic & Desire* and founding editor of *Brevity*

"In this collection of short moments chosen from a life of confusion, resentments, mistakes, epiphanies, friendship, loss, and laughter, Deborah Sosin traces the bumpy path to becoming who she is now: a woman complete in herself—imaginative, curious, full of life, and, perhaps best, someone she can rely on. Anna Hall's illustrations are marvelous, perfect. I loved this book."

—**Abigail Thomas**, author of *A Three Dog Life* and *Safekeeping*

"Combining the psychological insight of a therapist, the sensitivity of a poet, and the skill of an expert storyteller, Sosin has pulled off a dazzling magic trick, capturing seventy years' worth of transformation in seventy meaning-packed moments. *Escape Velocity* is a shimmering ode to the strength of the human spirit, and to the surprising ways our constraints can set us free."

—**Nicole Graev Lipson**, author of *Mothers and Other Fictional Characters*

"With the tactile skill of an old-world artisan, Deborah Sosin has conjured a wide-ranging palette of miniature vignettes for *Escape Velocity*, each with the vivid tone and luster of a colorful mosaic tile. And she has assembled these precise singular fragments into a cohesive self-portrait of a life journey that is both intimate and far-flung, glistening with themes of independence, love, loss, sexual awakening, psychological constructs, family ties that bristle and bind and evolve with the author's emerging self-awareness."

—**Robbie Gamble**, poetry editor at *Solstice Literary Magazine*

"In spare, illustrated morsels infused with psychological insights, Deborah Sosin unfurls a moving, later-in-life coming-of-age story that will resonate with many—especially those who have struggled to untangle themselves from complicated family dynamics and limiting societal expectations."

—**Sari Botton**, author of *And You May Find Yourself... Confessions of a Late-Blooming Gen-X Weirdo* and editor-in-chief of *Oldster Magazine*

"Sosin's beautifully precise seventy-word entries are expansive, deeply thoughtful, and often very funny explorations of the moments that shape a life. Generous, heartbreaking, and evocatively illustrated by Anna Hall, *Escape Velocity* reminds us of the transformative power we hold when we tell our own story."

—**Hester Kaplan**, author of *Twice Born*

"In *Escape Velocity*, Deborah Sosin's crystalline seventy-word micro-memoirs chart a decades-long journey to liberated selfhood, proving that freedom—hard-won and glorious—can arrive at any age."

—**Darien Hsu Gee**, author of *Allegiance* and *Other Small Histories*

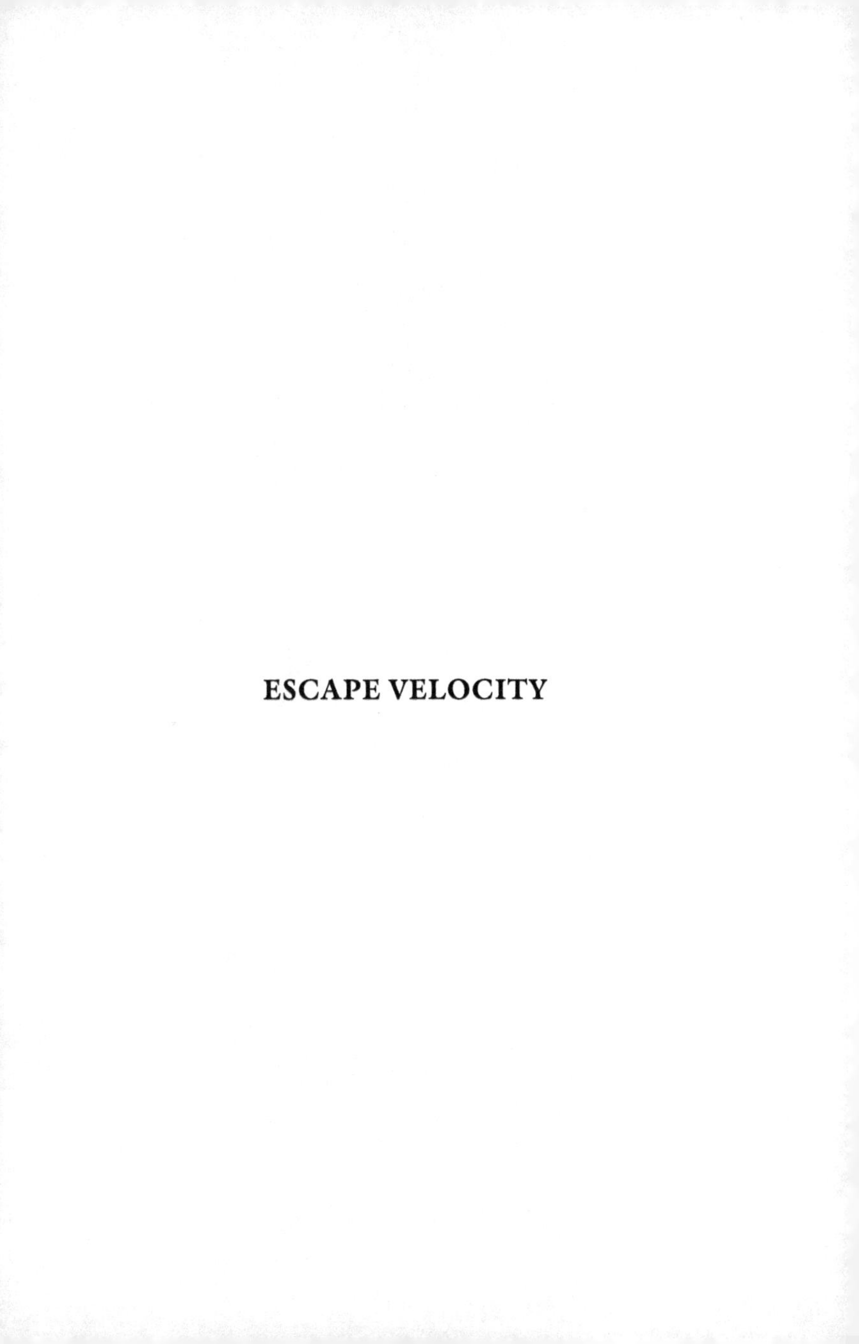

ESCAPE VELOCITY

ESCAPE VELOCITY

How One 70-Year-Old
Push-Pulled Her Way Out of Her
Too-Much-Not-Enough Family

70 MICRO-MEMOIRS, 70 WORDS EACH

Deborah Sosin

Illustrations by Anna Hall

To my legion of therapists, who guided me toward seeing and loving my true self. It took a while, but I got there in time to enjoy the view.

Contents

Prologue

1

IS THIS SEVENTY?

I could've sworn I left the lights on, but our house is oddly dark. I unlock the door, flip the hallway switch. "Surprise!" My grandchildren line up for squishy hugs. My children whoop, "Happy Birthday!" Dear friends circle round. And my bearded, dapper husband, iPhone in hand, records it all: potluck extravaganza, homemade songs, keepsake slideshow. I drink in loving toasts and tributes to a life well lived. My life.

2

FEBRUARY 27, 2024

None of that is true. Not the house nor my fantasied cast of characters nor the surprise. The reality? Still restaurant-phobic post-Covid, I cancel my annual birthday bash with my beloved posse of writers, musicians, therapists. Instead, on a shockingly spring-like day, an impromptu picnic with one old friend: flowers and doilies, shrimp and linguine, swirly chocolate cupcakes. Later, I toss together a Zoom with what's left of my family.

Part I

3

NUCLEAR FUSION

"Four-way kiss!" Mommy announces, arms extended, beaming. Daddy, brother Donnie, and I rush into our after-dinner huddle—forehead to forehead, noses rubbing, *mwah!* Daddy looks funny without his glasses. Mommy smells of Calèche perfume. Donnie scrunches his eyes.

On Sundays, we snuggle together in their double bed. I plop onto Daddy's bent knees, facing him, clutching his hands, waiting for the "surprise" leg collapse: "All of a sudden, Debbie goes...*BOOM!*"

4

HOME SICK

I have a miserable cold but I'm only half-miserable because staying home means Lovey Mommy instead of Naggy Mommy. Campbell's tomato soup placed on a saucer with a perfect saltine circle, brand-new Venus colored pencils, a single-stem red rose. She checks for fever, smooths Vicks VapoRub onto my chest, sings Yiddish lullabies. Even though I'll miss Sandy's birthday party, I sniff and cough louder for one extra day. Maybe two.

5

SUMMER RASPBERRIES

Daddy scooches his towel closer after swimming at Rye Beach. "I'm gonna give you the treatment!" he teases, moving even closer, smooshing his face into my belly.

"Wheee!" I squeal. I'm three or four. My bathing suit is a pink crepe-y one-piece with skinny black straps.

Pbbbt, pbbbt, he raspberries, tickling my under-arms, my feet.

"Stop, Daddy, stop!" I say, giggling.

Pbbbt.

"Stop, Daddy, stop!" I say, not giggling.

Pbbbt.

6

MY PERSONAL JUKEBOX

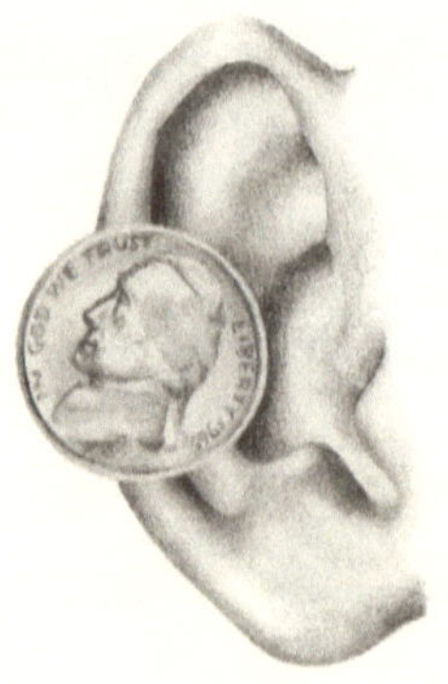

I extract an imaginary nickel from my pajama pocket and insert it into Donnie's right ear. "Play 'Where Is Love?'" I command. I'm ten. He's twelve. Cranking his arms like a robot, Donnie strikes the piano keys as I sing, then he slowly winds down. Another nickel: "'Please Please Me.'" More nickels, more songs. Broadway, folk tunes, Schubert Lieder. Mommy and Daddy bicker in the kitchen. We crank our volume.

7

AND NOW FOR A PSYCHOLOGY INTERLUDE: SALVADOR MINUCHIN'S THEORY OF ENMESHMENT

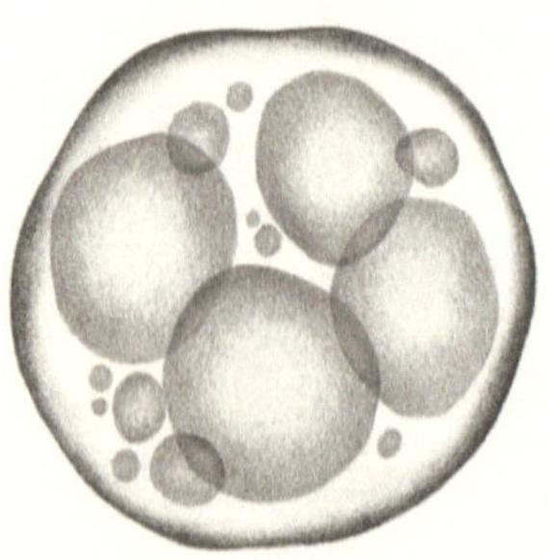

Think blurred boundaries. A sloshing blob of cells within a rigid, impermeable perimeter. What's mine is yours: space, bodies, thoughts, achievements. Minuchin's "emotionally incestuous" family system.

Thick in the ether of my childhood, inhaled from Jewish grandparents who fled tsarist Russia seeking safety, an implicit mandate: WE HAVE EVERYTHING YOU NEED. YOU'RE SURROUNDED WITH LOVE. STAY CLOSE, STAY LOYAL, AND WE SURVIVE. IF YOU LEAVE, ONE OF US MIGHT DIE.

8

TOO SOON

Not-so-well-hidden copies of *Kama Sutra*, *My Secret Life*, nudie postcards.

Overheard jokes at Mom and Dad's dinner parties: *boobs, tits, jugs*.

Ogling and va-va-vooms.

Playboy centerfolds dot Donnie's wall.

Obligatory wet lip-kiss greetings at family gatherings.

At twelve, Mom's birds-and-bees talk, featuring the precise choreography of intercourse and oral sex. And slang: *blow jobs, sixty-nine, cum*.

Her message? "Sex is *marvelous*!"

Her other message? "Wait till you're madly in love."

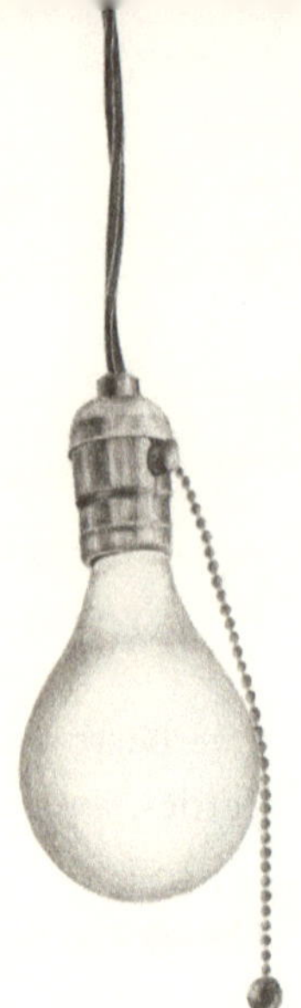

9

BOSOM BUDDIES

Inside my bedroom closet, lit by a bare bulb, my best friend, Priscilla, and I survey our "boobies," astonished at our longed-for markers of womanhood. We Scotch-tape ALL THE WAY WITH LBJ campaign buttons onto our nipples and pretend to be exotic dancers, gyrating, hip-thrusting for a nightclub full of adoring men. Later, while playing strip poker with the neighborhood boys, we stand up, circle slowly, slowly around, eyes lowered.

10

I NEED TO MAKE YOU SEE,
OH, WHAT YOU MEAN TO ME

Slow-dancing to "Michelle, ma belle" with not-too-bright Jerry at my sixth-grade party in our backyard. I've longed for brainy Robby forever, but he's making out with cheerleader Lynn. So when Jerry kisses me, I kiss him back.

Over the years, Dad, oozing melancholy, insisted on singing those Beatles lyrics to me. I'd cringe as he recalled gazing out the dining room window at his little girl growing up, growing away.

11

SCRAMBLED SIGNALS

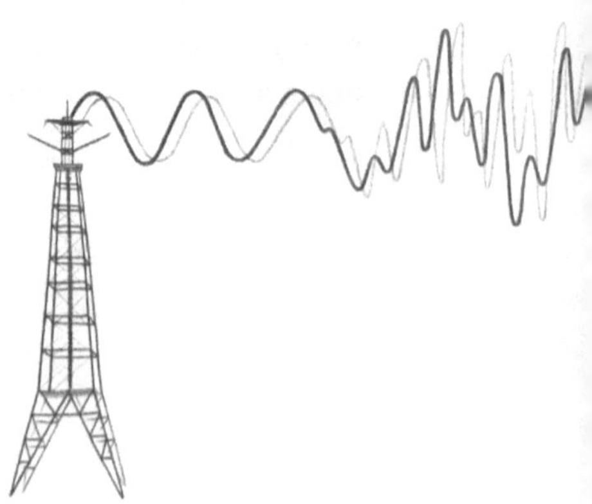

Dad's work with Radio Liberty catapults us from New York to Munich for four years. New country, new life. Severed from stateside family and friends, the four of us fold in even tighter. New clashing, too. My puberty and Mom's menopause. Sometimes, she compares our naked bodies: "We're twins!" Dad admires my "cute little figure." Then, when I model a clingy poor-boy sweater, he mutters, "You look like a whore."

12

SEVENTH-GRADE LOVE
IS THE PUREST LOVE

Freckle-faced, strawberry-blond John. Hallway notes, kissing at the Munich American High basketball game. And poetry! "Ice cream is cold, chili is hot, some girls are conceited, I'm glad you're not."

Holding hands, heads touching during *Fantastic Voyage*. "Will you go steady with me?" he murmurs. We vow not to tell our parents. His silver ID bracelet warms my pillow. *I feel so secure!* I tell my diary. *It's TRUE LUV!*

13

DEAR DIARY:
MARCH 1, 1967

uck! They found out! I can't keep John's ID cuz it's "too personal." They don't want me to get that "involved" with "strange boys." What the hell are they worried about? It's not like we're getting engaged or anything! I gave the ID back. Now John's with Jackie, of all people!

Well, this is the old bag spinster signing off.

Luv, Deb

PS: Fuck Mommy! I hate Mommy! Screw Mommy!

14

SYNCHRONICITY

Surrounded by folding maps, Dad and I eagerly plot the route for another family adventure—this time, Venice. Traversing the Alps in our trusty Peugeot, we sing Bach chorales, play Jotto and Botticelli. Our perfectly harmonious continental quartet.

Not long ago, I discovered a photo of Mom and me on the Rialto Bridge and stopped cold: we're sporting identical cat-eye sunglasses and custom-designed purple-and-yellow sleeveless shifts, our arms perfectly aligned.

15

DEAR DIARY:
DECEMBER 31, 1968

News: Triumph of Apollo 8. Israel and Arabs clashing. Paris peace talks moving along. I hope 1969 brings peace on earth—although I doubt it. Resolutions?

- *Resist smoking. (Build feminine willpower.)*
- *Grow, damnit!*
- *Quit swearing so much!*
- *Be demure—looks, attitude, actions.*
- *Continue interest in world.*
- *Send article to* Seventeen: *American girl living abroad!*
- *Write a book?*
- *Try to establish better relations at home, especially with mother—be less close?*

16

CAUGHT

Thank God Mom and Dad are busy hosting one of their lavish dinner parties when I arrive home from skiing in Garmisch, still high from ingesting mystery pills a friend casually offered. I dash upstairs, vowing never to touch drugs again.

Days later, the Grand Inquisition—lectures, accusations, scary anti-drug articles. *How did they know?* When Mom quotes exact sentences from my stoned-out diary entry, I get my answer. Grounded.

17

ORBITAL DRIFT

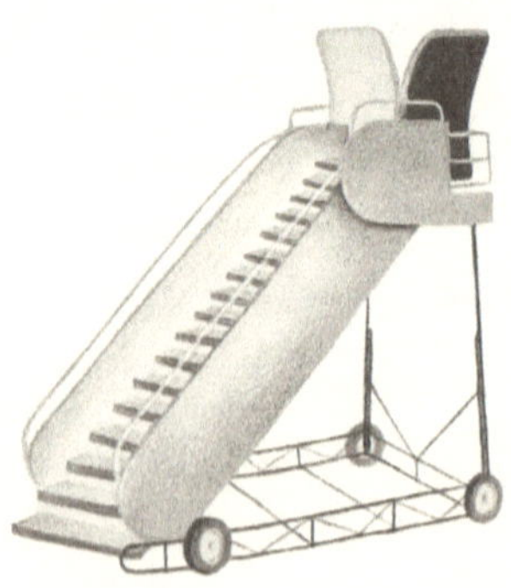

July 21, 1969, 3:56 a.m. Crunched together watching German TV, we cheer Armstrong's giant leap. Heart pounding, stomach flip-flopping: moon fever...and memory-rushes of last night's backseat smooching with bearded-beaded Heinrich. Around noon, I meet my buddy Elaine at the park. Popping our bikes onto the curb, we howl, "We have liftoff! Prepare for trans-sidewalk injection!"

August 14: Donnie flies off to college in Michigan. Suddenly a trio, not a quartet.

18

SOPHOMORE SOCIAL STUDIES

Franco walks me home through Perlacher Forest after flirting in class. Sweet, easy kisses. Then *bam*! He pins me down, yanks my jeans to my ankles, climbs on top. "When rape's inevitable, relax and enjoy it," I'd heard. I flail, babble, pretend I'm tripping-level stoned. He stops.

He probably thinks I'm frigid, I write. *I still want him! What's wrong with me? I'm a slut.*

I never tell a soul.

19

ESCAPE VELOCITY

hate the USA. Stupid teenybopper seniors.
Incessant arguments with parents. *Get me out.*

If I graduate midyear, spend six months in
Michigan, tuition's cheaper. *Please?* They
approve! *If* I live with Donnie till school starts.

March 4, 1972:

Ann Arbor! Turned 18! Apartment's great!
Donnie's away!
Killed cockroach—itchy ever since.
I like the freedom but not the loneliness.
I plan to meet Mr. Right in the laundry room.

20

PSYCHOLOGY INTERLUDE: ERIK ERIKSON'S THEORY OF PSYCHOSOCIAL DEVELOPMENT, YOUNG-ADULT EDITION

Behold Erikson's model for understanding the psychological life cycle: we face eight "crises," each with an existential question and ideal outcome.

The early-adulthood crisis, Intimacy vs. Isolation, asks: Are you capable of forming a healthy, mutual partnership? If yes, your outcome is love. Woohoo! But if you're dragging around unresolved crap from earlier crises, like infancy's Trust vs. Mistrust? Oy.

I had no idea, yet, what I was dragging around.

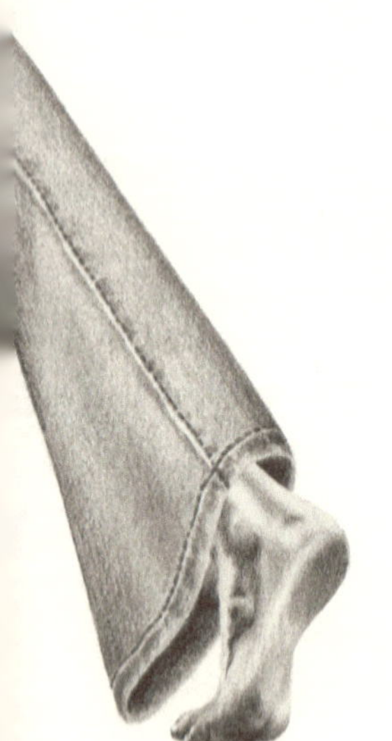

21

TRADE-OFF

Hell-bent on losing my virginity before freshman year ends, I follow Greg upstairs after the dorm dance. He's drunk. I'm sober.

I slide my diaphragm in. No kissing.

Poke, push.

"Ouch."

"You OK?"

"Yeah, go ahead."

Johnny Carson's monologue on TV. Blood.

Greg finishes, then passes out. When he wakes up, he slurs, "You still here?"

I dress quickly, slink to my room.

Mission accomplished—minus Mom's "madly in love."

22

THE DANCE

S teve: tenor, eighteen. Me: soprano, nine-
teen. Our souls collide over Joni, Barbra,
Sondheim. And, *swoon*, Brahms. When his
hunky boyfriend, Ken, isn't around, we make
out. And more.

Steve confides that once, while I wrestled with
my diaphragm in the bathroom, he stared at
photos of ballet dancer Edward Villella to stay
aroused. I want all of Steve. But he can only
offer me parts. So I settle for parts.

23

PIROUETTE

chase, wait, ache for more than "soulmates," more than Steve's occasional concession to make love. For two years, a tease, a torture, but I'm hooked. *He'll never change*, I remind myself. *He's GAY!*

One winter morning, my best friend, Laura, confesses she's sleeping with Steve. His fucking men is one thing, but fucking another woman, fucking *Laura*? I end our friendship. I should've ended it with Steve too, but...Brahms.

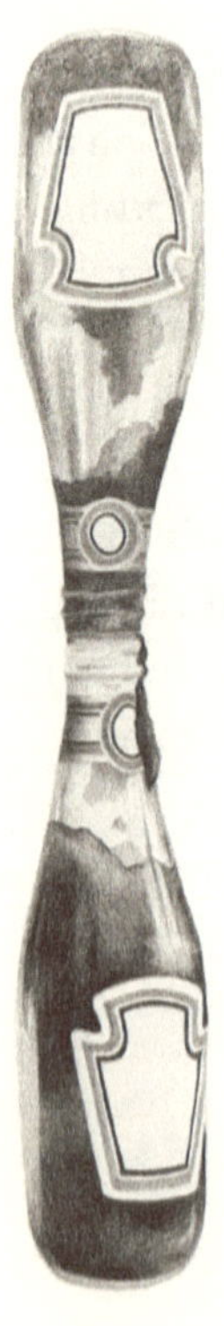

24

MY BODY,
MY SELF

Campus ignites with Roe v. Wade, the ERA, birth-control access. My apartment-mates and I pore over *Our Bodies, Ourselves.* Digging the wardrobe: army pants, baggy T-shirts, no bra.

Fuck "demure." Fuck objectification. *It's Ms., not Miss, Mr.*

But, at my restaurant job, scruffy-haired Wyatt flirts while we marry ketchup bottles after closing. I covet his Mark Spitz–like swimmer's body. Fuck feminism. I'll bat my damn eyelashes if I want.

25

CLIMAX

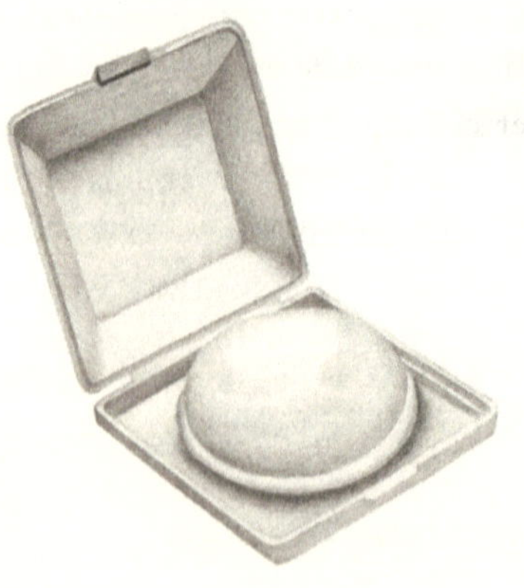

I don't mind Wyatt's scratchy beard sliding along my thighs. He can take me whole, take me half, breathless, boisterous, sweaty, tangling beneath my red Indian-print bedspread. At the crucial moment, I picture my diaphragm in the bathroom. *Shit. I don't want to break the mood. And what are the chances?*

Nausea. Tender breasts. Wyatt agrees to pay for half the abortion. No shotgun marriage. Just an explosive one-night stand.

26

DENOUEMENT

"Are you sure?" the Planned Parenthood counselor asks.

"Yes."

I'm only twenty-one. Plenty of time for kids.

Over the whirring of the vacuum's suction, the nurse squeezes my hand. I vomit from the Demerol.

Afterward, no tears, no regrets. Just relief among the circle of women I join, relaxing in orange recliners, sipping juice.

Steve drives me home and plays me Ravel and Fauré and Debussy until I fall asleep.

27

SEEN

Home for spring break. I refuse to share the Sunday puzzle with Mom. Can't I do *something* by myself?! Screaming match. The inner dam bursts. Gushing tears. Mom disappears upstairs. Dad hugs me awkwardly.

That evening, I spill my story to some big-deal psychoanalyst, a family acquaintance they'd called.

"Am I crazy?"

"No. You need therapy," she advises. "And don't tell your parents anything, even if they ask. Therapy's *private*."

28

**PSYCHOLOGY INTERLUDE:
MARGARET MAHLER'S
THEORY OF SEPARATION-
INDIVIDUATION**

An infant evolves from the merged ego-state with mother, then starts exploring. At "rapprochement," the toddler toddles merrily away but retreats when she senses, "Uh-oh, where's Mom?!"

Recently, I unearthed my first therapist's intake form requesting a "vivid memory":

> *I'm three. My parents were going on vaca-tion. I pounded the door, watching them leave, agonized. "DON'T GOOOOOO!"*

Rereading, I notice my vague syntax: *Agonized.* Who? Me? Them? All of us?

29

DESTINY OR DEFAULT?

Still waitressing after college, I'm lost. I head to Boston to find myself. Kelly Girl assigns me to a children's psychiatric clinic, where I type therapy reports thick with family dysfunction, devolution.

"You're wasting your talents! What about a career?" my parents implore.

Three years later, my boss echoes them, adding: "You'd make an excellent social worker."

I probably would. And I'd make Mom and Dad proud. Might as well.

30

COMMENCEMENT

Days after my MSW graduation, I'm gut-punched by Alice Miller's *Prisoners of Childhood: The Drama of the Gifted Child and the Search for the True Self*: Sensitive, attuned children develop a "false self" to meet the emotional demands of their insensitive, unattuned parents. They bury their needs and feelings…and many become gifted therapists. Now I understand. I'm not in this field to heal others; I'm in it to heal myself.

31

GRAVITY

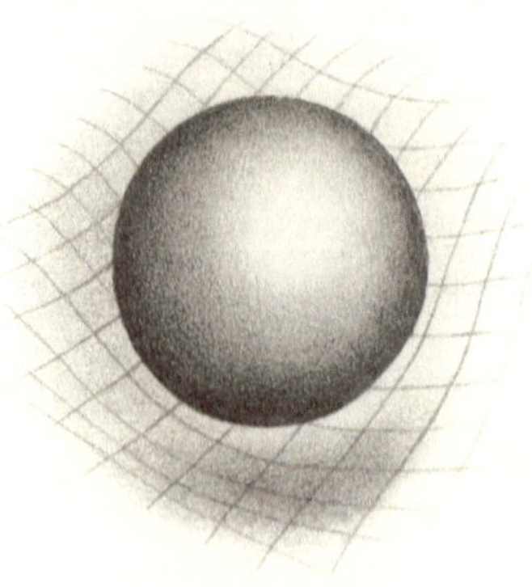

"I'm staying in Boston for Thanksgiving," I declare, summoning a boundary-setting strategy I studied in Family Systems: *Don't ask, tell.*

"What?! Everyone's coming!"

A full-scale family-wide campaign ensues. Phone calls, letters.

I celebrate with good friends instead. But, surrounded by their drunk relatives and too-loud Christmas Muzak, I'm tugged by an invisible force field—picturing Mom's festive table, the laughing, singing. The familiar, familial.

I'm twenty-nine. Where do I belong?

Part II

32

THE INTERPRETATION OF A DREAM

On the night of my thirtieth birthday, I dream I'm a child, climbing onto my parents' bed. They're cuddling, naked. Mom smiles, invites me to nurse. Her breast is a rubber diaphragm with a brown nipple. I open my mouth. Suddenly, with a dramatic swish, she pops off the breast. They exchange a knowing look, laughing.

Just that morning, my therapist said, "You grew up in a mirage of intimacy."

33

UNWANTED TOUCH
(PARTIAL LIST)

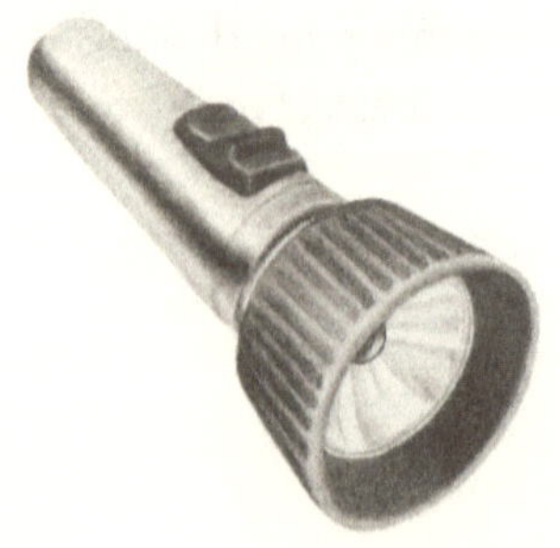

Hotel elevator operator: tongue-kisses my eight-year-old mouth.

Smelly stranger, crowded bus: presses his hardness against my side.

Tollbooth attendant: swipes my palm slowly while returning quarters.

"Uncle" Harold, parents' friend: pinches my "cute little tushy."

"Doctor" Charlie, fifth-grade classmate: probes my "privates," flashlight in hand.

Vincent, babysitter: fondles my budding breasts, sometimes.

Mother: kisses me on the lips, often.

Father: hugs me too tight, always.

My body remembers.

My body.

34

MY TURN

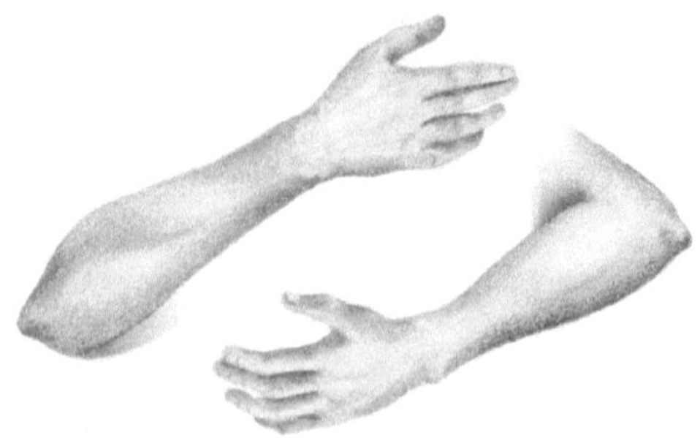

At a women's Healing the Inner Child retreat, I stumble through my story. My family's too-muchness-not-enoughness. Love. Confusion. Multiple shrinks who suggested fathers will tickle and ogle. Mothers will kiss and pry. Men will pinch. Boys will probe. "What's so awful?" "You're oversensitive." "You weren't *raped*."

Our earth-mother leader interrupts: "What happened to you *was* awful—it counts."

Nobody's ever acknowledged that before. I weep in her soft, strong arms.

35

PSYCHOLOGY INTERLUDE: DONALD WINNICOTT'S THEORY OF TRANSITIONAL OBJECTS

Think binkies or blankies. Transitional objects help babies as they withdraw from the mother and navigate the post-breast world, providing a soothing substitute for the brand-new "me/not-me" realm.

I bought a pudgy Teddy bear at my first retreat. Decades later, rips in her fabric expose white stuffing. Her black-button eyes and nose are scratched, her mouth one thread. I once thought about stuffie surgery, but I can't sleep without her.

36

PARTING WAYS

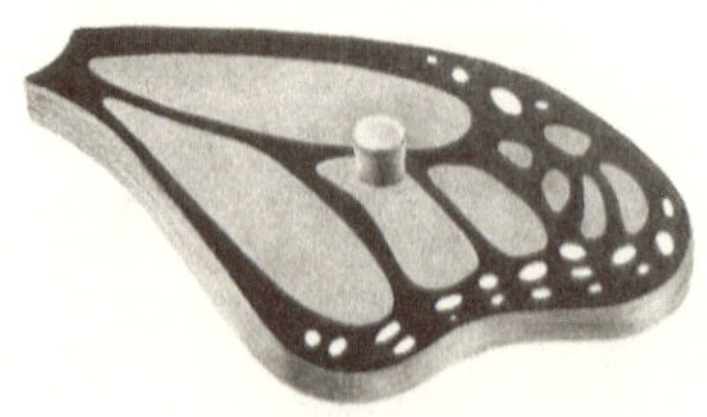

Edging toward burnout, I quit my therapy job with abused children and begin teaching at a Montessori school. Joy among exuberant toddlers lurching toward independence.

One morning, I join Pippa's distraught mother observing her distraught daughter through the one-way window.

"Can't I go hug her?" she begs.

I touch her shoulder. "Wait."

Within seconds, Pippa, gripping her Doggie, pulls out her favorite butterfly puzzle, her wails now slowed to sniffles.

37

IN FOR REPAIRS

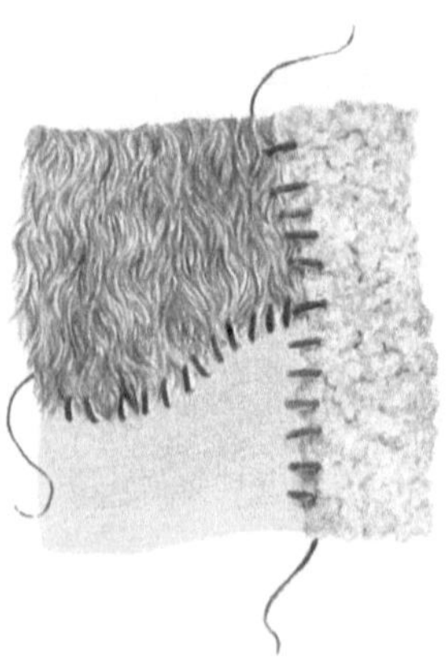

Another, less senior, therapist might have refused my request outright or insisted on analyzing it—grist for the mill, transference reaction, liability concerns, all that crap—but when Dr. R, having consulted his wife, also a therapist, allowed me, also a therapist, to curl into his lap, pillow under my head, Teddy against my chest, his hand firmly on my back, we discovered that some boundaries could be safely crossed.

38

CARE PACKAGE

My inner child craves parental space. I call "time-out." *No contact*. Reluctantly, they agree.

Weeks pass. A box arrives: bunny slippers, too-small tops, a *Cathy* cartoon that stings:

> "I'm in a horrible phase with my mother. I love her, I need her...but when I'm with her I'm defensive, cranky, and impossible...."

The punchline? Cathy's "phase" started at birth.

I return it with a scrawled note: "MOM! YOU PROMISED! NO CONTACT!"

39

POWER SURGE

I'm walking down a deserted sidewalk at night. A man approaches, grabs me from behind. "Don't move or I'll kill you." I whip around, jam his chin with my palm, unleash three full-thrust knee-to-groin kicks while screaming "NOOOO! NOOOO!" He reels, collapses. I bolt, shouting "9-1-1!" Hoots and applause from my Model Mugging classmates. High-fives from the heavily padded Mugger. I strut to the gymnasium sidelines, awaiting the next scenario.

40

RE-VISION

After a months-long time-out, I'm ready-ish to see my parents—at a family-therapy session.

I detail their intrusion and ignorance. And my sense of suffocation and invisibility.

Stricken, they apologize. "We didn't know, dear."

Is their remorse enough? Does it matter?

I see them: their flawed, familiar love. Can they see the real me? Doubtful.

Maybe what matters now is that *I* see me. I *see* me. I see *me*.

41

PSYCHOLOGY INTERLUDE: JOHN BOWLBY'S THEORY OF ATTACHMENT

Just because you're attached to someone doesn't mean it's healthy. Bowlby labeled different attachment styles "secure," "anxious," or "avoidant." The more secure the early bond, naturally, the better shot at forming mutual adult relationships.

My musical soul connection with Steve accordioned in college. Yes-no. Stop-go. I called it love then. Now thirty-five, I'd call it anxious attachment. And nothing, no one, since. Am I terminally avoidant? Or, worse, terminally unlovable?

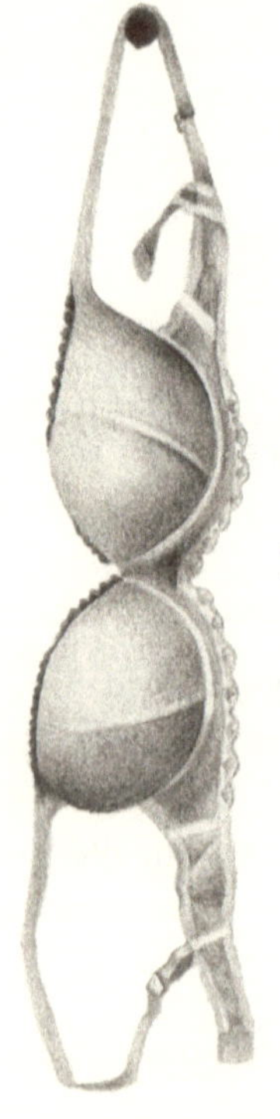

42

DEFROSTING

Day One: Co-ed, clothing-optional Discovering Intimacy weekend. Pairs of all sizes and shades form two concentric circles. Most are naked, sharing "love" histories. I'm clothed, frozen.

Day Two: I dare myself—bra and panties. I exchange stories with a meek, nude seventy-year-old man.

Day Three: Wildly curious, I shower with two buff young guys and a multi-tattooed transgender woman. We soap-splash and sponge-slather, giggly as children at a water park.

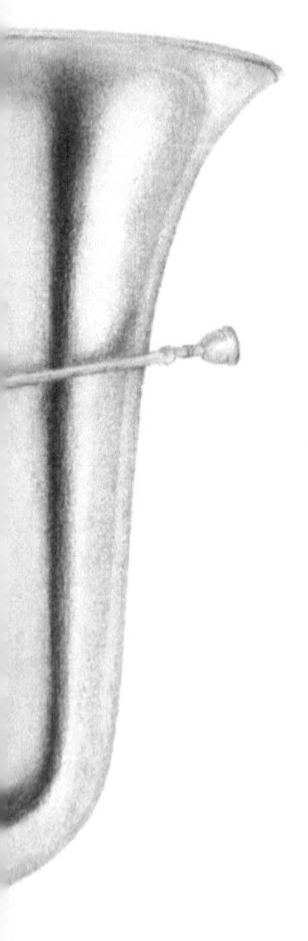

43

IT'S ABOUT TIME

Daniel: *Jeopardy!* champ, virtuoso brass player, virtuoso tongue. Weekend sleepovers, mixtape swaps, late-night Denny's. I'm thirty-seven and I can say "my boyfriend." He even meets my parents. But, at forty-two, he wears his varsity jacket, lives with his mother. And, like a vampire, sleeps all day, stays up all night. For six months, I stagger through his schedule. He yawns through mine. Alas, our incompatible biorhythms eclipse our scorching sex.

44

TWO-STEP BACKWARD

For my uncle's sixty-fifth birthday bash, I buy a slinky pink-and-gray dress that reveals my newly slim figure. But Dad's voice still reverberates: "You look like a whore."

"Do I?" I ask my therapist, modeling the outfit in his office ahead of the event.

"No. You look lovely!"

At the party, Dad approaches. "May I have this dance?" Delightful waltz! But he presses too close, too long. I freeze, again.

45

HYDROTHERAPY

Shaken from the waltz, I attend another Inner Child retreat. One night, I slide into the jumbo-sized Jacuzzi, hoping no one's looking, judging. Soon I'm immersed in slow-motion bubbles, lulled by the jets' lonely hum. Without my glasses, I recognize only swaths of naked flesh, no faces. Even so, I see them: my sweet, wounded sisters soaking our tender, hopeful bodies. Canopies of ficus stand like sentries in the mist.

46

HOLDING PATTERN

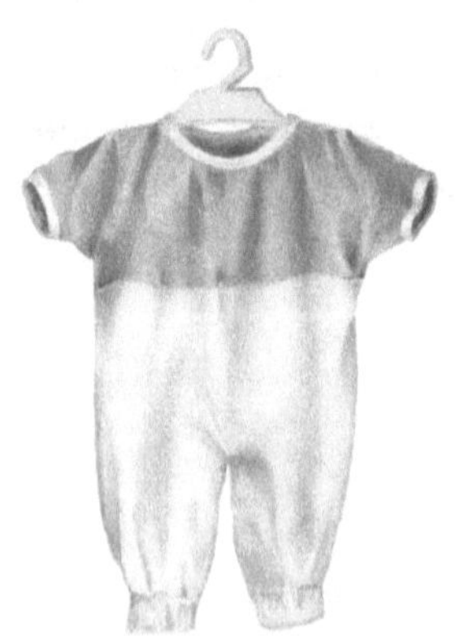

buy a brushed-cotton, blue-and-white onesie as a baby-shower gift for Roxanne, who ends up having a girl. And blue is strictly taboo for girls. More friends' showers—still no boys. By then, I've fallen in love with the outfit, so I keep it for myself: robin's-egg blue top, white collar, white cuffs, white bottoms, tiny snaps dotting its inner seams. I'm pushing forty. Will it ever be my turn?

47

WISHUS INTERRUPTUS

His rented Rolls-Royce barely squeezes into my guest parking space. Swooping in monthly from Denver, Richard, editor colleague, loves swanky restaurants, lavish bouquets. I'm forty-five, he's thirty-nine. I love our long-distance repartee—erudite, erotic. But the sex? Tolerably vanilla. "There's no greater pleasure than the male orgasm," he proclaims. So, when he finds a twenty-ish woman who'd *bear him children*, I'm hardly disappointed to leave his pleasure in her hands.

48

DISCOMFORT ZONE

Strolling by the river—*BOOM!* Heart pounding, throat closing. *I'm dying!*

"Premenopausal panic attacks are common," my doctor pooh-poohs. "Don't worry."

Are you kidding? I cocoon at home.

My therapist assigns daily walks: five minutes out, five back. Add five minutes weekly. At first, I count-breathe, watching my watch, watching my feet. By thirty and thirty, I'm rocking Motown on my Walkman, swooning over dogwoods.

A paint-chip-sized Xanax helps too.

49

PEAK EXPERIENCE

At a crossroads in Murg, Switzerland, I park my rental car, unfold my map. Mountain pass or superhighway? Traveling solo to Paris after seeing old friends in Munich, I've promised myself (and my therapist): risk over safety, adventure over caution.

Barely breathing, I navigate the spectacular Klausen Pass—treacherous hairpins, no guardrails. Climbing, climbing, no turning back. At the summit, I pull over and whoop into the fresh alpine air.

Part III

50

OPEN SPACE

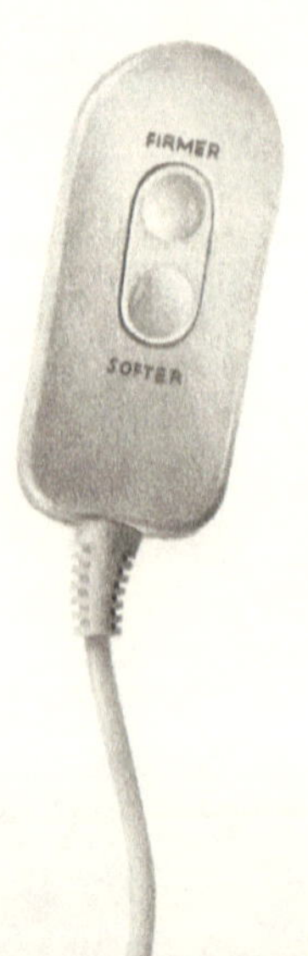

My full-size mattress dies. Saggy, lumpy, impossible.

I order a queen-size Sleep Number—his-and-hers airbags, his-and-hers remotes.

Night One, I plummet into a center trench.

"You need a partner's countervailing weight," the phone rep says.

"But the salesman promised..."

"Ah! We call you 'The Hopefuls.' I'll send a single-bag replacement—you can upgrade anytime."

"And the second remote?"

"Keep it for now," she says.

"Just in case," we both chirp.

51

THREE BLIND DATES,
SEE HOW I RUN:
MARK, THE HAIRY POLITICO

Kickstand Café: White ponytail, divorced, politically active, jazz musician. Potential!

In a monologue, he reveals his sister's hysterectomy, father's phlebitis, lackadaisical coworkers, socialist leanings. He finally asks, "You're a therapist and a writer—what do you write?"

I begin.

He interrupts.

I go pee, ponder my options. *Give him a chance.*

When I return, he still rambles.

"I have to leave," I lie.

He says, "Let's do this again sometime!"

52

**THREE BLIND DATES,
SEE HOW I RUN:
ANTHONY, THE CLOSE
WALKER**

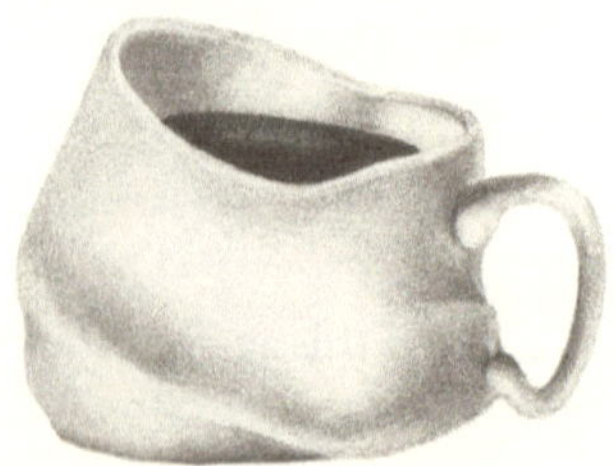

Fresh Pond: Divorced songwriter. Sweaty hug. Margarita, his chihuahua, yips.

As we walk, his bristly arm hairs tickle. I edge away. He edges toward. We rest on a bench. His thigh grazes mine. *Give him a chance.* He confesses he's five years older than his profile. Sixty to my fifty.

Margarita pees on my brand-new capris.

"Sorry, I've gotta go!" I say.

Anthony calls out, "Let's do this again sometime!"

53

THREE BLIND DATES, SEE HOW I RUN: LAWRENCE, THE SINCERE DEPRESSIVE

Starbucks: Lanky health administrator, meditator. Chinos, checkered shirt. His gastrointestinal history, three ex-wives. Asks no questions. *Give him a chance.* We touch on depression and death, diverticulitis and diarrhea.

After an hour, he says, "Let's evaluate our date!"

I say I need time to digest it.

"My best in ages!" he says.

I decline a second date but earn his endorsement: "Your future partner's a lucky guy."

I quit dating.

54

OLD BAG SPINSTER LIFE

- Total responsibility for TV choices, mealtimes, bathroom access, ventilation, thermostat, cluttered vs. clean
- No conversation when I don't feel like talking
- No demands for hugs, kisses, sex
- No one whose needs I must meet

- Total responsibility for shopping, cooking, cleaning, dishes, cat care, laundry, bills
- No conversation when I do feel like talking
- No requests for hugs, kisses, sex
- No one whose needs I might *want* to meet

55

SIXTIETH-BIRTHDAY REVERIE

imagine leaning over and whispering to my twenty-one-year-old self, the one at Planned Parenthood. "So, Deb, guess what? Turns out this will be your one and only pregnancy. No true luv, no husband, no kids. Do you want to change your mind?"

For the first time, I wonder, *Was it a boy or a girl? What would my child have been like? Would I have been a good mother?*

56

IT'S A BOY

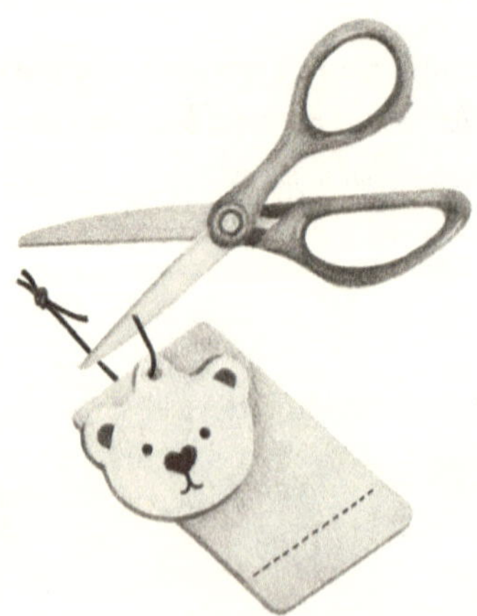

Closet purge every April. I'd always spot my onesie and sigh, fingering the upside-down OshKosh B'Gosh bag on its tiny hanger. One spring, my downstairs neighbors have a son, Jackson. Big ears, goofy smile. Is it time?

I lay out my onesie, carefully snip off the labels, soak it in Woolite. After twenty-plus years, it deserves to be washed. On the card, I write, "This onesie comes with a story."

57

PSYCHOLOGY INTERLUDE: BUDDHISM AND MINDFULNESS

The Buddha lived 2,600 years ago but, dang, did he ever nail that meaning-of-life stuff: the inevitability of suffering. Impermanence. The futility of grasping, clinging. The antidote? Practicing awareness with curiosity, compassion, and acceptance. Right here and now.

At a spirited Seder, finally edging beyond the force field's pull, I admire Dad's razor-sharp wit and storytelling prowess, Mom's unflagging energy and Jewish-mama warmth. Cherished in-jokes. Five-star musicale. And now-welcome hugs.

58

THE HALF-LIFE OF BLISS

At a mindfulness weekend, after rounds of yoga and meditation, energy cascades through my body-mind. Four a.m., wired, I study my reflection: *Whoa. The physical manifestation of my SELF!*

Driving home, I'm one with the windshield and the highway and the foliage, one with every vibrating molecule on Earth. Two days later, raking leaves, still rhapsodic, I think, *If only this could last forever.*

Poof. Gone. The grasping, my undoing.

59

UNSPOKEN

I always imagined naming a daughter Charlotte, after Dad's mom, who died when I was eight. In my late-life MFA program, I birth a picture book, *Charlotte and the Quiet Place*, where Charlotte finds inner peace through mindful breathing. It sells! Dad eagerly drafts an atrocious sequel. *FUCK OFF!* I think. But, invoking my lovingkindness strategies, I reply, "Thanks, Daddy. Love your enthusiasm! Stay tuned." We never mention it again.

60

AFTER ALL, IT WAS DADDY WHO...

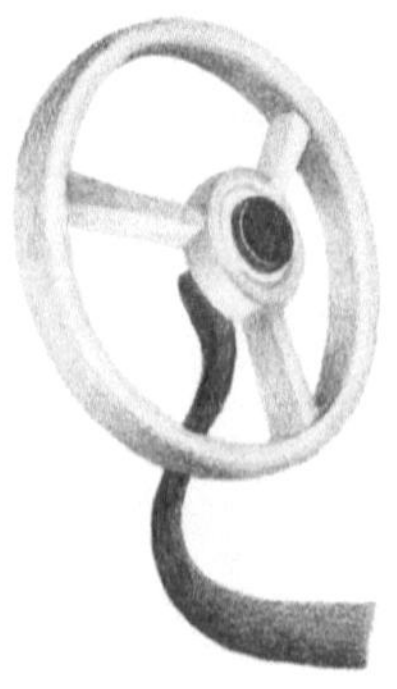

R ocked me to sleep, humming, "Ah-ah-
ah-ah, baby."

Installed a car seat with a big red horn and let
me *beeeeeeep.*

Balanced me on our lawn mower's crossbar.

Nudged my Royce Union two-wheeler until
I finally soloed on Ormond Place.

Cheered when I mastered stick-shifting our
Peugeot.

Waved goodbye as I headed for college in the
clunky Rambler.

Hung in for our long, bumpy ride, even when
I drove him away.

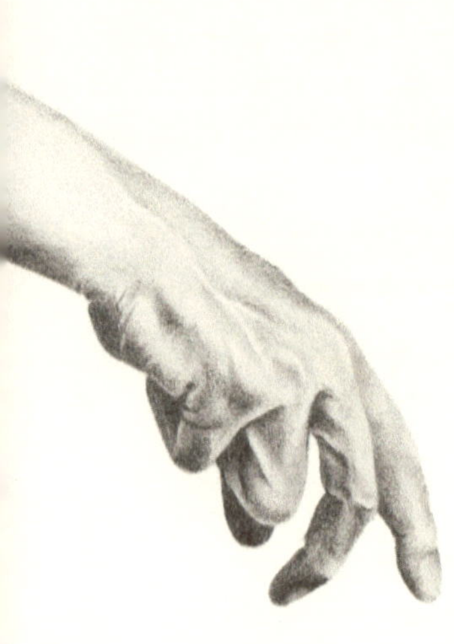

61

G-O-O-D-B-Y-E

Dying of aspiration pneumonia and tethered to a ventilator, Dad, ninety-three, communicates by finger-tracing, letter by letter. I show him my hot-off-the-press advance copy of *Charlotte*. L-E-A-V-E B-O-O-K, he spells. For the ICU staff, so he can *kvell*.

On Dad's final Friday, Donnie and I light Shabbat candles, sing "Shalom Aleichem." Dad mouths the lyrics, eyes alert. "What's on your mind, Daddy?" I ask, stroking his forehead. L-O-V-E, he answers.

62

AND NOW A PAUSE FOR
A TEENY-TINY RANT,
THANK YOU VERY MUCH

Mom refuses to consider assisted living. Ever.

Donnie and I long-distance manage her money-pit house.

And her devoted but high-maintenance aide, Natasha.

And ulcer-inducing troops of Medicare bureaucrats.

Then Trump. Lockdown. Pandemic. Blahblah.

Apparently delusional, I'd envisioned my sixties as carefree, creative.

Instead, I call Mom nightly, visit monthly, absorb her—and Natasha's—woes.

For six years.

An inheritance? Hahahahaha.

Fuck mindfulness. Fuck lovingkindness. I never signed up for this!

63

WHO WILL HAVE ME NOW?

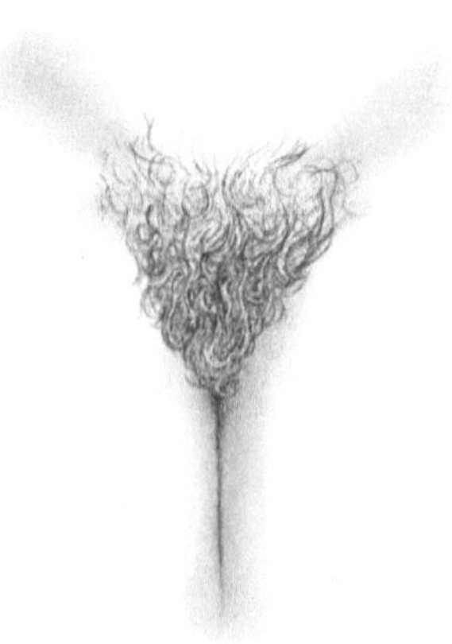

My face sprouts moles. My once-jaunty breasts slouch toward my thickening waist. My pubic hair is grayer, thinner. Nine crowns, one implant. I sleep with a mouth-guard, wrist brace, orthopedic pillow. I'm lactose intolerant, allergic to scents, battling insomnia.

Diagnoses: osteoporosis, tinnitus, arthritis, carpal tunnel, hyperthyroidism, IBS, reflux, dry eye, dry skin, dry everything. I ask my doctor about sex at my age. "Lots of lube," she says. "And patience."

64

MAGIC QUESTION

Feather-frail at ninety-eight, Mom struggles to stand, even with my support, as Natasha deftly changes her diaper. Five years a widow, she's survived fractures, pneumonia, heart surgery.

"Great job!" I say, squeezing her hand.

"Thanks, dear."

I used to hate when she compared "our" cheekbones, crooked second toe. But today, if I asked a Magic 8 Ball, "Am I turning into my mother?" it would answer, "Signs point to yes."

65

RECKONING

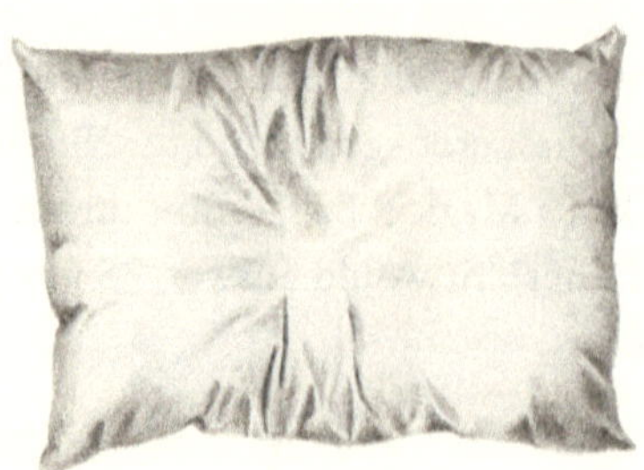

When I see Mom fetal-curled on her deathbed, and it looks like it really is her deathbed now, not just another dress rehearsal, and the nursing-home doctor confirms that her body really is shutting down, that, no, she'll never wake up, and it's only a matter of days, or hours—something in me shifts. I'm flooded with waves of...what? Relief? Regret? Grief? Rage? Forgiveness? Love? Acceptance?

Yes. All of it.

66

LOSS FOR WORDS

For his eulogy, Mom's longtime rabbi asks for adjectives.

"Umm," I say.

"Umm," Donnie says.

"Yeah," the rabbi says, laughing along with us. "I know."

We begin: critical, narcissistic, grandiose, entitled, controlling, intrusive...which clears the way for: whip-smart, caring, fashionable, musical, erudite. Generous to Soviet emigres, fellow breast-cancer survivors, strangers. Russian and Yiddish translator. Published writer. Fabulous knitter, hostess, apple-pie baker.

She was exactly ninety-nine years and three months old.

67

NOW WHAT?

Monarch butterflies travel from Canada to Mexico without a map. Instinct? Compulsion? Spiders trap, raindrops drown, millions die. Survivors cluster for months before returning. How would it be to set out on a preordained path, persist without deliberation, obey one's destiny despite dangers? Sometimes I'm overwhelmed by possibilities. Sometimes I'd like to soar like a butterfly on a thermal wind, no thought, no feeling, just moving toward whatever lies ahead.

68

PSYCHOLOGY INTERLUDE: ERIK ERIKSON'S THEORY OF PSYCHOSOCIAL DEVELOPMENT, SENIOR EDITION

The after-sixty-five life crisis: Integrity vs. Despair. Have I found meaning? Fulfillment? Or am I regretful, disappointed? Erikson's existential question: Is it OK to have been me?

Stashed in the bedroom closet, scores of dusty diaries: my life in a box. Sometimes those marvelous, angsty chronicles beckon: *Come look, learn, remember, reflect!* Sometimes they sneer: *What was the point, anyway?* Who will want to know my story when I'm gone?

69

THIS IS SEVENTY

Zoom party with what's left of my family:
Donnie, sister-in-law, nephew, niece,
two cousins.

Cacophonous "Happy Birthday!" popcorning
across frames.

Donnie's surprise—a whirlwind "DebFeb27"
slide montage: dainty to mod to hippie, pig-
tails to Twiggy-pixie to stick-straight glam.

Place-bouncing through Munich, Venice,
Paris, Athens, London. Stellar European
extravaganza.

And everywhere, sparks of the elders—
vibrant, youthful, ever-so-continental.

Mom would've said, "Carpe diem."

Dad would've said, "Goes by in a flash."

70

WHAT IF SONDHEIM GOT IT WRONG?

"Alone is alone, not alive." I heard that lyric again recently, from the musical *Company*.

Instead of my familiar longing-sobbing, I thought, *Hey! I fought hard for alive and alone.*

Not alone-lonely.

Alone-separate. Alone-free.

Donnie once said, "You're a radiant being—you'll find someone."

Yes, I'd love to love, be loved, somehow…

be alone-free *and* together-attached, someday…

But love or no love, I've got my self, my radiance. Expanding. Abiding.

Acknowledgments

Over the almost two years from conception to completion of *Escape Velocity*, I was fortunate to have extraordinary readers and supporters. Heartfelt thanks to Cindy House's ultra-insightful class for your early comments. To my picture-book buddies, Audrey Day-Williams, Jenny Lacika, Betsy McGovern, and Mia Wenjen, for saying, "Yes! Do it!" To the amazing Cambridge Common Writers for cheering me on at Lesley MFA alumni readings.

Much gratitude to Leah Hager Cohen, Grace Coventry, D. Dina Friedman, Leah Glennon, Nicole Graev Lipson, Sandra Miller, Julie Wittes Schlack, and Allison K Williams for deep-dive beta-reads midway. Many thanks to late-stage readers Deb Fitzler, Peggy Freudenthal, Liz Gray, Holly Hartman, Jayne Yaffe Kemp, Carol Ober, and Elyse Pipitone. To Marcie Kaplan for our long talks about memoir writing. To Amy Yelin, fellow writer-explorer, for your friendship. To Suzanne Hanser for your wisdom and warmth. And to my honorary sister, Susan Rubin, for your sharp design eye.

Utmost appreciation to my dream team of endorsers: Sari Botton, Robbie Gamble, Darien Hsu Gee, Hester Kaplan, Nicole Graev Lipson, Dinty W. Moore, and Abigail Thomas. Your gracious words touched me to the core. And to Sari Botton and Hattie Fletcher for publishing excerpts in *Oldster Magazine* and *Short Reads*, respectively.

To Steve Moebs, my soulmate—I cherish our long, long friendship. Thanks for agreeing to let me tell our story. Luvya (and Brahms) always.

To Donald Sosin, my brother and jukebox: We've survived the push-pulls of our siblinghood for seven-plus decades. I'm grateful for our friendship and abiding love and for your enduring support of my creative work. And to what's left of our family: Joanna Seaton, Nicholas and Mollie Sosin, Nancy and Bobby Hirschhorn, and new member Kathryn Engelhardt—love you so much.

To Anna Hall, whose powerful *Short Reads* illustration for "Bosom Buddies" was the catalyst for our happy, unexpected partnership. Enormous thanks for your boundless cheer, flexibility, and vision. Now I can't imagine this book without your artistic voice, which shines through in each drawing and in the stunning cover and design. What a blessing.

Finally, this book exists because of my brilliant developmental editor, Michael Lowenthal—brother from another mother, spiritual counselor, mentor, partner in word counting and verb tweaking. You saw a throughline emerging from my random snippets. Despite my wavering, you nudged, guided, and inspired me to write the deeper story. Zoom by Zoom, email by email, syllable by syllable, you showed up with intensity, patience, humor, and genius-level literary sensitivity. GRATITUDE. (This is 70. ♥)

Escape Velocity Crowdfunder Heroes

Out-of-this-world gratitude to everyone who so generously contributed to my FreeFunder campaign to support the publication of this book. (Donations received after January 27, 2026, are listed at www.deborahsosin.com.)

Benevolent Booster (under $70)

Anonymous
Jacqui Bloomberg
Sari Botton
Joanna Cooke
Katie DeBonville
Jodi Sh Doff
Dorian Fox
Irene Stern Frielich
Ethan Gilsdorf
Liz Gray
Suzanne Hanser

Jeff Ikler
Maria Judge
Jill Johnson
Maida Korte
Julia Leef
Brian Lies
Richard Lindo
Judi MacKenzie
Betsy McGovern
Jerry Minkoff
Jen Minotti

Deb Olshever
Pam Pacelli
Pam Petro
Diane Pienta
Julie Wittes Schlack
Elise Church Schmidt
Amy Sokal
Nancy Stolarz
Mia Wenjen
Phyllis Wilner

Liftoff Champion ($70+)

Anonymous (2)
Gile Beye
Grace Coventry
Barbara Gaffin
Robbie Gamble

Josh Gordon
Jenny Lacika
Nina McGehee
Sandra Miller
Steve Moebs

Elyse Pipitone
Ginny Rowan
Jill Sandberg
Teri Thompson

Gravity Breaker ($140+)

Nancy Hirschhorn
Diane Shufro
Robin Stein

Intergalactic Orbiter ($210+)

Anonymous (2)
Babette Trout Dammon
Donald Sosin

A Word on Word Count

According to my research, software engineer Richard Brodie likely deserves credit for introducing the word-count function around 1985, in the early days of Microsoft Word. Without that happy (or often confounding) little counter on the bottom left of my screen, I couldn't possibly have tackled this project.

For the curious, to arrive at exactly seventy words, I stuck to whatever the counter said. So, all hyphenated words (like "too-muchness-not-enoughness") counted as one. Same for words separated by an ellipsis and no spaces ("word...word"), which offered me some breathing room without worrying about cheating. I loved that moment of seeing "70," knowing I was done...until the next round of revisions, that is.

About the Author

DEBORAH SOSIN is a writer, editor, clinical social worker, and GrubStreet instructor. Her essays have appeared in the *New York Times, Boston Globe Magazine, Brevity* Blog, *Cognoscenti, Salon, The Manifest-Station, Oldster Magazine, Short Reads*, two anthologies, and other publications. Her picture book, *Charlotte and the Quiet Place*, won the Gold INDIEFAB and Silver IPPY awards, among other honors. She is also the author of the *Sober Starting Today Workbook*. Debbie earned an MFA from Lesley University and an MSW from Smith College School for Social Work. She lives outside of Boston with her cuddly tortoiseshell cat, Lini. More at www.deborahsosin.com.

1958, Fourth Birthday

2024, Seventieth Birthday

About the Illustrator

ANNA HALL is a book designer and illustrator based in Seattle. Over the past eight years, she has worked with self-publishing authors, small businesses, and independent publishers across all genres. Anna is co-founder and illustrator of *Short Reads*, an online literary magazine publishing flash nonfiction, and previously served as art director and designer at *Creative Nonfiction* magazine. She studied visual art and earth sciences at Bowdoin College. When she's not making books, she's often making elaborate dinners for friends. More at www.annabhall.com.

www.ingramcontent.com/pod-product-compliance
Lightning Source LLC
Chambersburg PA
CBHW022054050726
47591CB00002B/531